Out of
the
Ordinary

Meditations by

Gordon B. McKeeman

Boston
Skinner House Books

Printed in Canada.

Cover design by Suzanne Morgan

ISBN 1-55896-401-0

Library of Congress Cataloging-in-Publication Data

McKeeman, Gordon B. (Gordon Butler), 1920–
   Out of the ordinary / Gordon Butler McKeeman.
      p. cm.
   ISBN 1-55896-401-0 (pbk. : alk. paper)
      1. Meditations.   2. Spiritual life—Unitarian-Universalist
churches—Meditations.   3. Unitarian-Universalist churches—
Prayer-books and devotions—English.   I. Title.

   BX9855.M39 1999
   248.4′89132—dc21

                                                99-058502

10 9 8 7 6 5 4 3 2 1
03 02 01 00 99

These pieces are
lovingly dedicated to
Phyllis,
my steadfast companion in marriage
for over half a century

CONTENTS

Before you venture further, may I tell you what my intention is in writing these pages? My sense is that many of us aspire to live more frequently in ways that are deeply satisfying. Sometimes we do feel as though we have experiences that hint at deeper dimensions of life. These moments are cherished and often recalled. They beckon us toward more such moments. But we are forgetful, occupied, preoccupied, even perhaps overoccupied—too busy.

Or we think these uplifting, inspiring moments depend upon being in extraordinary surroundings: in wilderness, on mountaintops, or at the ocean's rim. Doubtless, being in touch with stunning natural beauty invites the spirit to soar. Many, however, have only infrequent contact with the extraordinary. We live in ordinary places, do ordinary work, discharge ordinary duties. So, to be able to find the extraordinary in the ordinary is one way to make each day—if not each hour or each moment—a life-enhancing occasion.

What I intend is just this: to point to the extraordinary that is present, awaiting our encounter with it. A friend sent me a note card whose front page showed a beautiful close-up photograph of a pond lily. On the back page was the message: "This photo was taken at an instant of time on an ordinary day.

Don't miss the ordinary, often it's extraordinary."
Pardon me, then, if I point to ordinary things and
invite your brief attention to the so much more con-
tained therein.

Many people have contributed ideas and sugges-
tions and have pointed out materials I wrote and sub-
sequently forgot. My selection for this assignment was
a surprise, albeit a very pleasant one. Marty Wilson
was the chief conspirator in submitting my name. My
fondest hope is that it meets the expectation of those
who were instrumental in my accepting the role. Of
course, none of them is responsible for the form or
content. The form is for others to decide. The content is my choice. It's ordinary stuff to offer a bit of
brightness for the ordinary days.

Gordon B. McKeeman
Charlottesville, Virginia

Ministry is

> a quality of relationship between and among
>   human beings
> that beckons forth hidden possibilities.

> inviting people into deeper, more constant
> more reverent relationship with the world
> and with one another.

> carrying forward a long heritage of hope and
> liberation that has dignified and informed
> the human venture over many centuries.

> being present with, to, and for others
> in their terrors and torments
> in their grief, misery, and pain.

> knowing that those feelings
> are our feelings, too.

> celebrating the triumphs of the human spirit
> the miracles of birth and life
> the wonders of devotion and sacrifice.

> witnessing to life-enhancing values
> speaking truth to power

standing for human dignity and equity
for compassion and aspiration.

believing in life in the presence of death
struggling for human responsibility
against principalities and structures
that ignore humaneness and become
instruments of death.

It is all these and much, much more than all of
them, present in
the wordless
the unspoken
the ineffable.

It is speaking and living the highest we know
and living with the knowledge that it is
never as deep, or as wide
or as high as we wish.

Whenever there is a meeting
that summons us to our better selves, wherever
our lostness is found
our fragments are united
or our wounds begin healing
our spines stiffen and
our muscles grow strong for the task

there is ministry.

My dictionary provided a definition of ordinary (number 9 of 16) that was something of a surprise: "a clergyman appointed to prepare condemned prisoners for death." As often as I have thought of myself as an ordinary clergyperson, that particular description was not any part of my notion about what I was (or was supposed to be) doing.

Now that I think about it more carefully, it may be as succinct and accurate a statement about ministry as any. Probably it won't be widely embraced because it contains words that don't come easily to our tongues: *condemned, prisoners,* and *death.* We don't really like to talk (or even think) about such things. Long ago our ancestors in the faith sought liberation from such concepts as *condemned.* The God they spoke of and believed in was a loving God, and loving meant not condemning anyone to an eternity of unremitting punishment—no matter what his/her shortcomings, sins, foibles, or deficiencies (including deficiencies of faith). Many of us consider the death penalty to be unacceptable—somehow compounding whatever heinous crimes the person has committed.

We're very attached to freedom as well. Prisoners have no freedom. They are restrained, presumably to protect the law-abiding, and possibly as an instrument of rehabilitation—although removal of freedom, by itself, seems inadequate for the complex process of rehabilitation. And our entire society eschews talk of death. Even hospitals, where death frequently occurs or is confirmed, seem to prefer euphemisms, as though it is unthinkable that anyone should die there.

Strange, then, that the person appointed to minister in such circumstances should be an Ordinary. But in some larger sense we are born here on earth, and we are prisoners here on earth. Death, it appears, is our only means of escape. Each one of us, as far as we know, will die—some while still young, too young to die, we say; some in the fullness of years; and some (it seems) after unnecessary pain and undeserved suffering. These are, whether we like it or not, the ordinary conditions of our lives, which we did not choose and which we can do little to alter.

We have discovered, however, that even in these ordinary circumstances there are extraordinary possibilities. Our limited engagement need not be simply "full of sound and fury, signifying nothing." We can, and often do, love. We can both create and appreciate beauty. We can contribute to others' joy, happiness, and contentment. We can hand on the gift of life, together with all its many opportunities. We can, and often do, struggle toward fairness, equity, compassion. Prisoners we are, condemned ultimately to death. Anyone can be an Ordinary, a herald of life and love, of compassion and joy. Ordinary indeed!

The other day I was driving on an expressway. These days expressway driving seems a frantic enterprise. Near one of the exit ramps, one of the highway denizens, a behemoth "semi" had pulled over onto the berm. The driver had emerged and was gathering some wild plants along the side of the road.

In that moment another stereotype bit the dust. I know what truck drivers are like. They are strong, burly masters of profanity, rootless gypsies who have neither homes nor families. They care not a whit for sunsets, mountain peaks, seashores, or wildflowers. But now I have seen one take the time to stop and look carefully at the splendor by the roadside. I've been by that very spot numerous times. Not once did I take the time or trouble to stop and look at the miracles of leaf and flower. Goodbye, shattered image! I think I shall not miss you at all! You were, it should be said, quite convenient. You allowed me the luxury of not having to think of truck drivers as real people, as varied as the vast diversity of wildflowers.

Stereotypic thinking does not impart solidity or dimensionality to an object. Quite the opposite: It dispenses with the details and eliminates the idiosyncrasies of individuals by making them members of a class of things, all of which have identical characteristics. Well, all truck drivers do have a common characteristic—they do drive trucks. That may exhaust the list of characteristics they share. There's one of them, at least, who notices what is growing beside the road. Quite a feat, actually, at seventy miles an hour.

As the number of people inhabiting our little globe grows, so, I suppose, will the temptation to group people into classes, apply labels to them, and mistake the label for the far more complex reality. Perhaps the image of the truck driver stopping to gather wildflowers by the side of the road can be a reminder of how perilous, how depersonalizing, how diminishing such stereotypes can be. I've had a number of stereotypes pasted on me. As I pause to think about them, I like my own name better than any one of them. I have a hunch that others like their names as well, far better than a label and far, far better than a number. The struggle to maintain a sense of importance for each of us may be long and often difficult. The challenge is quite extraordinary every ordinary day.

I frequently encounter invitations for regular check-ups. Both my doctor and my dentist suggest when my next checkup should be scheduled and are prepared to make appointments and send reminders. I remembered earlier today to look at the furnace filter, which needs to be cleaned or replaced regularly to assist the heater in operating at peak efficiency. The auto mechanic reminds me to check the coolant in the radiator. So do the autumn leaves.

It occurred to me that my religion might need a regular checkup. If my body can develop problems of which I am not made acutely aware by some pang, pain, or pressure, I suspect my religion can, too. Early tooth decay proceeds without palpable warning. The furnace filter becomes clogged silently. So, too, my religion may be needing a regular examination—a checkup.

What kind of pulse-taking would be appropriate? Doctors, dentists, auto mechanics have records. When was the last service performed? The doctor wants to know if I'm still taking medications, how much, and how often. The dentist checks on the regularity and thoroughness of my flossing. I wonder why ministers avoid asking when I was last at worship or whether my daily devotional practice is as regular as ever. And does that mean, really, daily or only occasionally—"when I feel the need"? My doctor wouldn't be happy if daily medications were taken on an "as needed" basis. And how are my religious reactions? Is my conviction about the supreme worth of *every* human personality being neglected? Am I succumbing to slurs on others and forgetting who are my sisters and brothers, my neighbors? Does my activity reflect a desire to win politically, economically, socially in ways that ignore or do violence to my religious convictions? How often do I forget that everyone is a child of God? When does it happen? When I read the newspaper accounts of drug-dealing, reckless driving, or ecological irresponsibility?

It just may be that the idea of a sabbath, one day in seven, was suggested (should I say "ordained"?) so that our religious life would be as well monitored and tended with preventive maintenance as are our teeth, tonsils, and transportation. Once a week doesn't seem too often. You never know when you'll need to have your faith in top-notch condition. I've also tried to bring the ministry of religion to many who have allowed their religion to atrophy. It's a very difficult task.

Unexpectedly, suddenly, there was someone out of the past—a person remembered, but not fully—a timbre of voice, a familiar glint of eye or shape of face or a distinctive mannerism. And then a name recalled, a summons sent down to the dim recesses of memory to call up the recollections of times past, events long faded into mists of years now gone, but not really gone. Rather years that have been put away to await the summons—to be called back to life.

Lurking there in the shadows are all of our pasts—all the ecstasies, the hurts and harms, the shames and prides, the successes and failures, the ghosts, the familiar figures that haunt our days and nights—summoned forth by sounds unheard to visit us with secret pain or solace.

It does seem strange that we who have such experiences so commonly think that immortality is only a fantasy, a figment of fond hopes that death shall pass us by. Nay, we shall live, the familiar spirits in lives beyond our own.

But since we cannot avoid death, it may be wise for us to consider what messages shall be elicited from our spirits. Will we be ogres from whom others shrink in fear or anguish? Or something more fondly remembered, sustaining with soft messages of love and joy, of courage and confidence, of acceptance and encouragement?

To think thus of ourselves and others recalls a statement attributed to Jesus: "Lo I am with you always." For our memories of the past are not easily brushed aside; nor are they quickly erased. One of the problems with which we wrestle is how to hear the old ghosts without allowing them to rule our future, as they have reigned in our past. While it is impossible to change the past, when the ghosts were real and regnant, it is not required that we surrender the future to their sway. Let them have their day, but yield not tomorrow. It belongs to the living.

Are not we all haunted houses, inhabited by spirits, by loved ones and unloved ones as well? How spooky, thinking of ourselves as ghostly shades called up when our name echoes down the halls of another's unconscious. If you're bound to be a haunting figure to another, why not a friendly ghost?

"Seeing is believing." I suppose so, but that's not
   all there is to it.
There's so much reality that is unseen, invisible.
   My living room is awash in things that arrive
      by routes invisible.
   The television set offers pictures of events
      transpiring half a world away—almost
      instantaneously—through the air and the
      space above it, often reflected (so I'm
      told) by satellite, also mostly invisible
         a flood, a famine, a volcanic eruption
         a coronation, a funeral, an inauguration
         a birth, a battle, a peace conference
         a festival—in full color.
   I don't see it in the air; I do, however,
      believe it, sight unseen.
Oh, but I must take my pills!
   That event launches another unseen process.
   How my body knows where to send all those tiny
      particles (so insignificant, save for the
      expense) to nourish, stimulate, hold in
      check, destroy, inhibit, heal, supplement
      is one vast, invisible process that eludes
      seeing, even seeing by microscopes.
   Not seeing, I do believe.

I drive my car and its radio plucks music, traffic
advisories, weather reports, the latest news
out of the ether on command. There's not just
one message lurking invisibly all about me, but
a whole catalog of choices to be selected by
the twist of a dial or the press of a button.
   I don't understand, nor do I see them, but
      I do believe.
Human beings, too, send messages that arise from
invisible wellsprings.
   I wonder whence cometh the tenacity, the courage
      the tenderness, the aspirations that are the
      invisible sources of perseverance, quiet
      bravery in the face of pain, love for those
      who are sometimes hard to love, hope that
      prevails over dark despair.
   Whence they come, I cannot see.
      But I do believe.
Some wise person once defined religion as an
invisible means of support. Fortunately, there is
great power arising from invisible sources.
May it be your good fortune on this quite ordinary day
to be able to believe in some invisible things that
have extraordinary consequences.

There are many relics in our home—objects to which important memories are attached. You probably have some, too. Each recalls some journey, event, or person that is a part of your life's experience. They're precious on that account—religious objects that summon up powerful recollections. One of my favorites is my tie tack. It's an opal, full of fiery iridescence.

The tie tack was an unexpected gift. Its former owner, the donor, came out of the church's worship one Sunday. As I greeted him, I noticed his tie tack and I said to him, "What a beautiful opal!" On the spot he took it off and gave it to me. I was both delighted and chagrined. I took off my tie tack, a UUSC flaming chalice, and gave it to him. It was far from an equal exchange. More important, what he did in that fleeting moment was very typical of him. He was a person of whom it could be said without exaggeration, "He'd give you the shirt off his back." He lived quite an ordinary life. He was a salesman of advertising novelties, so he spent much time in his car traveling from client to client. He spent a significant portion of his driving time thinking of ways to improve the community. He could be counted on to suggest some modest and simple change that would make a positive and real difference in people's lives. Some of his ideas were real winners, saving much public money and touching many lives with joy and opportunity. My life was one of those.

One of my joys associated with wearing a necktie is to put on my tie tack. I have quite a few of them, but my opal is always my choice. It's a ritual. I put it on and remember the man who gave it to me, and I resolve to find in this day some opportunity to continue what was his real life's work: doing something simple, modest, and useful to improve the life of the community.

Over the many years I have worn my tie tack, many people have admired it. To many of them I have told the story of my acquisition of it and of what it means to me. With each telling I have confessed that I ought to give it away, since that's how I obtained it—by admiring it. Some day I know I will give it away, together with its story. Meanwhile I say that I'm keeping a list of its admirers and offering to add the name of another possible recipient. Meanwhile, I keep wearing it and keep reminding myself of its meaning in my life.

Reflecting on one's relics now and then is a useful spiritual discipline—remembering the events, the persons, the occasions when ordinary things were somehow transformed into religious objects. All around us are the reminders of the days of our lives, the people whose touch was a blessing, a balm, an invitation, a beckoning to be a better person—deeper, more secure, more daring, more generous, more caring. My tie tack does more—much, much more—than hold my tie. On some ordinary day like today, I invite you to consider your relics.

In 1977, Dr. Seuss, famed author of children's books, was chosen to be the commencement speaker at Lake Forest College. He began his address by explaining that he had been researching the function of commencement addresses and had concluded that the speaker should give graduates all he knew of the world's wisdom. This is his speech in its entirety:

> My uncle ordered popovers from the restaurant's bill of fare. And when they were served, he regarded them with a penetrating stare. Then he spoke great words of wisdom as he sat there on that chair: "To eat these things," said my uncle, "you must exercise great care. You may swallow down what's solid. But you must spit out the air. And, as you partake of the world's bill of fare, that's darned good advice to follow. Do a lot of spitting out of the hot air. And be careful what you swallow."

We are regularly invited to swallow great quantities of hot air claims for the efficacy of a vast variety of products, guaranteed to have this or that felicitous result: softer skin; fewer wrinkles; presentable toenails; overflowing reservoirs of energy; relief from every manner of pain or discomfort, no matter what its origin or location. Results are assured; your money will be refunded if you are not completely satisfied.

Such claims are but a token of the problem. In many realms there are people working diligently to conceal the truth, to mask the truth by speaking only a part of it, or to persuade that the truth is not being perceived correctly, and putting a "spin" on it to assist in the truth-seeking process. One result of this outpouring of exaggerated claims, distorted information, and untruths is that communication becomes much more difficult and the truth of what one is told is seriously eroded. In the old fable, the boy who cried wolf when no wolf was present was deprived of his own safety because those who might have saved him didn't believe his cry of "wolf" when a real wolf appeared.

The obverse side of this coin is the responsibility of the hearer to be willing to receive a truthful message. Much hot air arises from the assumption that a listener cannot stand to hear the truth in its plain, unvarnished form. Unpleasant reality is often concealed lest hearers be upset. Hearers, however, are often doubly disturbed upon discovering the unpleasant truth and, in addition, the deception involved in hiding it.

"The truth in love" is a lofty standard to uphold. Every ordinary day offers opportunities to be a teller and a hearer of the truth. Wrote Universalist divine

18 Hosea Ballou, "If we agree in love, no disagreement can do us any harm. If we do not agree in love, no other agreement can do us any good." Hot air is fine for heating, but it contributes little to the quest for light.

What it says about inadequacy, futility, insignificance!
   A drop in the bucket. What's the sense? What's
      the use?
We're no longer in the center of things.
   Copernicus removed the earth from the center
      of the solar system. Darwin removed humans
      from the center of the earth. Astronomy has
      removed the solar system from the center of
      the universe.
Well, who are we, then, and where are we?
   Physiologists call us "weak, watery solutions,
      more or less jellified."
   Mark Twain said, "Man [sic] is the only animal
      that blushes—or needs to."
Just suppose that we are the merest drops in a bucket.
   There are unspoken assumptions here.
   We assume that a full bucket is what we're aiming at
      and that until the bucket is full, nothing has
      been accomplished.
   There is never a shortage of buckets. The empty
      bucket litany is long and tedious: racism,
      sexism, ableism, authoritarianism, oppression,
      injustice, violence, environmental degradation,
      overpopulation.

You feel like a drop in the bucket? Who asked
you to *fill* the bucket—especially all alone?
Remember how many there are who share your
concern. We may feel daunted, but we are not
one drop. A sense of isolation is the parent of
the drop-in-the-bucket feeling.

Sometimes one can decide the size of the bucket.
Don't think you can do a large bucket? Try a
smaller size. Even imparting a bit of hope—
a pat on the back, a financial contribution, a
few hours of volunteer service—every drop
helps!

It might even be wise to remember

why you need to help fill *this* bucket, possibly to
quench the thirst of someone hard at work on a
larger one

that buckets of whatever size are filled a drop at a
time. If you don't help, it will take even longer.

that your drop may be one of the last ones needed.
(Why is it that our image is of the first drop in
the bucket?)

where we'd be if everybody gave up putting drops
in the bucket—probably much worse off.

Persistence depends on patience, on keeping at it
when there is little to reassure us. It would be too
bad to give up, to sit back, bemoan the sorry state
of the world and wonder why somebody, anybody,
everybody (but not me, thank you) doesn't do
something about "it."

After all, the Grand Canyon was fashioned by
  drops of water,
    as ordinary as they seem.

When I was a child, one of my favorite toys was a gyroscope, a weighty wheel suspended in a cage on an axle. Winding a string around the axle and pulling the string would start the wheel spinning rapidly. When the wheel was spinning, the gyroscope resisted efforts to change its position. It could be perched precariously on a sharp edge or on a length of string and maintain its position. Later, I discovered that gyroscopes had other, more important functions than entertaining children. Keeping ships at sea on an even keel was one of them.

Still later, when I was an active parish minister, someone once described my style of ministry as gyroscopic. I gathered that this person noticed that I tried to keep the church on an even keel and moving forward by trying continuously to balance the emphases of the church's programs: stressing social responsibility when we were very busy with personal faith issues and reminding members of personal religious disciplines when we were absorbed in social action.

Now I'm very much occupied with maintaining my own personal equilibrium. This is true physically. I try hard not to fall. Older folks are often seriously injured in falls. But there's much more to it. I also have diabetes, and blood glucose control is an important health measure. In this area, again, balance is important. I also try to keep abreast of current events, a field in which equilibrium is seriously challenged because of the turbulence of our times. Probably you cherish equilibrium, too, for reasons similar to mine.

The most intriguing aspect of the gyroscope is that it works by spinning rapidly. This rapid rotation in a fixed location creates resistance to moving away from that plane. If the wheel ceases spinning, its resistance vanishes and it is easily moved to any position.

It occurs to me that my religious faith, the wheel of core convictions in my life, has to be moving continuously if I am to keep my balance, mentally and spiritually. Friction and gravity operate to slow down the gyroscope's wheel. Likewise, if I do not keep my faith going steadily, it may well lose its ability to keep me on an even keel, thereby protecting me from being overwhelmed, capsized by the turmoil and tumult around me. A regular pause in the day's course to check my gyroscope is important to me. You never know when some gale, hurricane, crisis, or tragedy will begin beating on your equilibrium, your peace of mind, your composure. Check your gyroscope. Make sure it's spinning serenely around your axle's fixed points.

In the gospel of Matthew, Jesus is reported to have said, "The very hairs of your head are numbered." Nowadays, when I pull out my comb, I am reminded that the calculation includes a good bit of subtraction in recent years. The consequence of that evolution is that I use my comb more often. This is a development that I had not anticipated. Shouldn't more require greater attention than less? But, indeed, the effort seems far greater now that there is less. Perhaps I should not be surprised that considerable work is required to get the greatest possible effect out of a limited resource.

Applications of this phenomenon occur to me often. We may all soon be learning the new artistry of making less do more for us and others. Less, rather than more, is likely to be a distinguishing character-istic. We may look back upon the present time, with its raucous shouts for "more! more!" to have been the last gasp of the few in a world of limited resources and an expanding population. It is a useful, but demand-ing, art: doing more with less, and being able to say *enough* rather than *more*. There was little challenge to making hundreds of hairs cover a single half-inch square. A few quick swipes and the job was done. Not so today. For each strand must pull its weight a hun-dredfold: no shirkers, no extra margin to conceal a hasty, slipshod job. Ah, but how gratifying when it comes out right.

The greatest art reveals no superfluity. The art of the sumi painter is to make each stroke of the brush count. The art of the Japanese flower arranger is to make every element play a role in the loveliness of the whole. Nothing extra, nothing that does not count.

Our material resources may not be the only aspect to benefit from this artistry of economy. Time also may be used in such a way as to make each fragment count for something. As the time remaining diminishes (as it does continuously for each of us), the consciousness of its slipping away adds impetus and urgency to time utilization. I note that the busiest people seem to have the most time. They use it with such care and artistry. Such artistry of economy may be a life-and-death matter, I am reminded as I take up my comb for one more swipe across the increasingly barren landscape of scalp.

Our camper van is one of the less active members of the family. It does a great deal of they-also-serve-who-only-stand-and-wait duty. It's reassuring to see the van there ready to burst into activity at the turn of its key, admirably alert for a vacation jaunt or a bulky load that would overwhelm our modest sedan. The other day, though, when our constant-duty vehicle was absent on errands, I needed to undertake what seemed an urgent mission. So I took to the van and turned the key. Nothing. Not a cough. Not a tremor. Not a flickering light. Nothing. My routine and instantaneous diagnosis: a dead battery. The battery was five years old, and it had probably died a slow death because of prolonged inactivity aided by the subtle and gradual drain of an unturned-off radio.

Once the local AAA service came and jolted the engine into unaccustomed action, a new battery was obtained and installed, and the faithful van was rehabilitated for further action-ready, patient waiting. It occurred to me that sometimes we leave our religions sitting idly in the corners of our lives awaiting some emergency—a crisis, accident, or untoward happening. Day by day, however, the depredations of our time have drained away our religion's power. Comes a crisis, we leap to our religion and turn the key. Not a whimper, a cough, or a shudder. No light flickers. Nothing.

Then we are reminded that a little preventive maintenance might have kept our faith energized for just such a time as this. That's one of the reasons that even a simple daily devotional practice and/or regular attendance at communal worship needs to be a part of our ordinary routine—it keeps one's religion in working order. It's no accident that my automobile mechanic suggests a weekly running of the van. Likewise, religious institutions offer weekly opportunities for the worshipful gathering of the faithful. It's to keep our religion in good shape.

We never know when an urgent need for our deep and active faith will arise. So it's a good idea to keep it in good shape. It's sad to see people who thought they had an active faith discover that it has lost its resilience through prolonged disuse. It looked strong as it sat there, but it had a dead battery. When people ask why I attend church so regularly, I respond, "I go to church to recharge my battery." I want to be as sure as I can that my religion will be ready to serve when it is most urgently needed.

An ancient Zen story tells of the master who poured tea into the student's cup long after it was already filled, to underline an important understanding that learning requires some emptiness. Unless there is an emptiness (sometimes called *yearning*), no learning is likely to occur. This suggests that, particularly among the learned, some unlearning is important.

It's hard to know how to encourage unlearning. There are probably many things that I now know aren't true, even though I believed at one time they were true. The ongoing quest for knowledge, when successful, makes the partial truths of the past less true, possibly even false. "New occasions teach new duties. . . ." Doctors now can do things once thought impossible. Engineers can, as well. People can expand their horizons beyond "my kind, my color, my language, my customs, my notions, my sexuality." The king in *The King and I* laments, "I wish I could be certain of the things of which I'm absolutely sure." The unchanging—the immutable—seems far more elusive than it once did.

In the last analysis, it is not knowledge for which we yearn, but wisdom. Surely knowledge and wisdom are kin, but in some significant way they are different. Put another way, knowledge offers us the key to "how to." Knowledge has opened doors to possibilities undreamed of in earlier times. The marvels of modern science and its twin, technology, are impressive, often even astonishing. The pace at which new knowledge is discovered seems to accelerate daily. Some even wonder if we ordinary folks are not suffering from the impact of "information overload"—knowing too much all at once.

It is more likely that the growth of knowledge, which we assumed would simplify decision-making, appears to be making decisions more difficult. Expanded knowledge increases our options and widens our horizons. In such a situation, wisdom plays an important role in our lives. Our dilemmas are not so much "how to"; they are "whether to." Even ordinary events present a bewildering array of choices: what to have for dinner, what toothpaste to use, what to wear. . . . Knowing the choices helps but little. Wisdom, fundamentally, is knowing who you are, where you are, and what you're trying to do or be. These are not matters of knowledge. They are matters of faith.

Choices in all matters, whether trivial or life-and-death, do not yield to knowledge. They require wisdom. The psalmist said, so many years ago when knowledge was very limited, "So teach us to number our days that we may apply our hearts unto wisdom." This petition becomes increasingly urgent as floods of knowledge threaten utter confusion. Even when it's only an ordinary day.

A decade ago Japanese Emperor Hirohito died. There was much speculation about his role in World War II. I wondered then, and I wonder occasionally even now, what his life must have been like. He did not choose to be Emperor; it was an accident of birth, a hereditary position. All accounts of his life describe him as retiring and shy, most at home in a biological laboratory studying various marine species. He wrote several books on the subject. As Emperor he had little actual power and enormous symbolic power. He took actual power only once, after the dropping of atomic bombs on Hiroshima and Nagasaki. When Japan's military leaders disagreed about continuing the war, he decreed a surrender. He said once that his fondest dream was to live just one day as a common person. His fondest dream!

Most of us live the Emperor's dream day after day. It may never occur to us that we are the daily recipients of what the Emperor could only vainly hope to have: a day as a common person. A common day replete with common things, the kinds of things we take so for granted:

> sleeping and waking again to a new day

> performing simple chores: dressing, making the bed, eating breakfast

reading (or seeing) the world's new terrors and
torments, tragedies, and triumphs

doing ordinary work, whose impact is largely
unfathomable but would be missed by someone
if it were not done: the laundry, cleaning, meal
preparation

looking out upon the ordinary world, breathing
the air, drinking the water, enjoying children
at play, marveling at the beauty of flowers, the
vastness of the sky, the gutsy heroism of simple
folk

remembering loved ones near and far: those
who have been our teachers; our companions
and acquaintances; our benefactors and
beneficiaries; our neighbors, even our ancestors,
who lived through common days, mostly hard,
and occasionally tolerable or easy

calling to mind those who bequeath color,
fragrance, and texture to each common day

recalling the vast fabric of love and labor
performed day and night by those unknown
to us, who make our lives easier

and a thousand more unmentioned blessings.

One who finds so many wonders and beneficences
in a common day understands deeply the line uttered

by Emily in Thornton Wilder's *Our Town:* "Oh, earth, you're too wonderful for anybody to realize you," followed by the anguished question, "Do any human beings ever realize life while they live it—every, every minute?"

Today is one common day, one (more) chance to be fully alive. Welcome to it!

My world? Not so.

I may be the world's
but the only part of it that is mine is that private
interior view I have of events, places, and people
the world filtered though my feeling, my hope
and, sometimes, my despair.

Its light and shadows are my knowledge and ignorance
Its height and depths are the geography of my soul
Its rain, my tears; its sunshine, my laughter.

I long sometimes to escape the prison of my being
to see things as they are
    and then I wonder if I am not safer
    in my own interior world, where facts
    can be molded and reality shaped to
    my own needs.

So, in the end, I safety enfold myself in my own
world chrysalis.

But, now and then
a shaft of out-there penetrates the in-here
    sometimes it is a wound
    sometimes a freshening breeze
    sometimes a hearth-brightening blaze

or a flash of light illumining for an instant
  the darkness of my self-prison.

Arise, prisoner in your dungeon-self!
  Tear away the bars
  Crumble away the concrete
  Melt the locks.

Trust yourself to the world.
It will possess you in the end.
  Let it have you living
  That it may cradle you dead.

Some time ago I expressed doubt as to whether or not Unitarian Universalism is really a religion. In response, the Rev. Dan O'Neal, then struggling with advancing cancer, wrote:

> I have often thought of UUism as a zero in mathematical terms. Now, I really *respect* the zero in math. It was a brilliant invention by Arabic mathematicians, a place holder which doesn't inject a specific content, but which holds the space as important. And yet, the human soul longs for that content, and is not satisfied ultimately with just a place holder.

Yes, of course, the space is important. Dan found it of great importance. When he left evangelical Christianity, he thought there was no religious option left for him. Unitarian Universalism offered him a religious option. He embraced it enthusiastically. But, important as it was, it became insufficient. He wanted (needed, he said) more.

I believe there is more. The long histories of our faith's traditions speak in an affirmative voice of our belief in human possibilities. They reject the notion that we are fundamentally sin-sodden, disobedient creatures bound for perdition unless divine intervention saves us. They reject the notion that human destiny may be either heavenly or hell-bent. Rather they see *all* of us bound together and with but a single fate. Despite our fumblings, failures, foibles, and faults, we still entertain the liberating conviction that we can live in peace on this globe, that we can learn the conditions of our survival soon and well enough to prevent the species from becoming extinct. We see the promise of humanity in its arts, its literature, its ideals of love and world friendship and community. We are not the only folk ever to have embraced such a hopeful vision of our future, and we are happy to join hands, hearts, and hopes with others who share these convictions of our possibilities. This is a long way from zero.

Zero is important, and it's an acceptable place from which to begin a religious journey. But it's not a good campsite. Moving on requires discovering what we believe about who we are, where we are, and what we're trying to do/be. It also involves reviving those convictions every day in the face of people and events that seem to derogate and devalue all that we believe. It's so easy to forget, so easy to be swept along in tides bent toward destructive and life-denying directions. The impulse toward wholeness is natural. But to turn its potential into the actual in day-by-day words and deeds on behalf of human possibility requires devotion, perseverance, and continuing commitment. That takes practice. A daily pause for refreshing our faith is indispensable.

Zero is important. But by itself it doesn't add up to very much.

Very early a few mornings ago, I fell out of bed. It was not—I repeat *not*—an ordinary event. I don't recall ever having done so before. And I hope I'll not do it again. Apparently, as I slipped over the edge, I made a desperate grab for something firm to prevent my fall. The night table wasn't it. It tipped, drawers slid out, and I bruised a knee on the corner of a drawer. It hurt. I was very uncomfortable, not a little chagrined, puzzled, a bit angry, and (need I say) unhappy. How did it happen? I didn't know. I wasn't en route to anywhere. I wasn't even awake until I began to fall.

Then I thought of a little squib from a church newsletter of at least a generation ago: "People fall out of church for the same reason that children fall out of bed: they fall asleep too near the place where they get in." That's the reason. I fell asleep too near the place where I got in. End of story? Not really. I began to wonder whether such accidents happen in other contexts.

There are many, many books that remain unread. I went to sleep too near the place where I got in. And there are many people I might have gotten to know better, listened more intently and purposefully to their stories rather than waiting for a pause so I could tell mine. I went to sleep too near the edge. I hear people talking about "living on the edge"—I suppose at the boundary between the known and the unknown. In some sense, we all dwell in that realm. Each new dawn heralds an unknown day. We sometimes assure ourselves that the new one will be similar to those we have already lived. We feel reassured by the hope of reliability.

My unexpected, disorienting, and discomforting fall out of bed has impressed upon me the conviction that the edge is not a good place to fall asleep. If you go to sleep there, you're likely to miss some great new happenings, like the ending of a conflict, a truce between old enemies, a new bit of community taking root in a casual acquaintanceship, or a new blossom sprung from an old plant. Of course, we must sleep. I can tell you it's not a good idea to go to sleep too near the place where you get in. The edge is an all right place, but it's not for sleeping.

The relationship between religion and health is an ancient one, going far back in human history to shamans, medicine wheels, incantations, and exorcisms. More recently, Mary Baker Eddy's Christian Science has attracted many adherents. Most Unitarian Universalists are more likely to consult a medical doctor than a minister about bodily ailments, although other forms of therapy have numerous devotees.

The relationship between physical health and the spiritual realm, however, has not disappeared. We are discovering that illness is more complex than we had assumed. Among the complexities is the insight that curing and healing, while related, are not the same. Curing has to do with the elimination of disease. It is the primary province of medicine and surgery. Healing has to do with a more inclusive view of the human being; it is related to the whole of life, not merely to the health (or the lack thereof) of an individual. The achievement of a whole (holy) relationship with all of life, healing is truly the province of religion.

These two realms, curing and healing, are not separate realms, but are rather a continuum with a shared boundary area. Here at the boundary are located the functional or psychosomatic ailments, those in which the body is made ill by the state of the mind or emotions. Likewise, here the mind is rendered less lucid by ills of the body. It is also in this area that the curative powers of the mind play a role in restoring the body's health, and the body's healthful trends clear the mind.

So we have four possibilities that may arise from the interplay between curing and healing. We may be both cured and healed, neither cured nor healed, cured but not healed, or healed but not cured.

Beset by incurable cancer, Judith Goodenough wrote a last letter to "neighbors and fellow creatures." In it she said

> I am writing from enormous pain and sickness and fever and fatigue. It does come to us sometimes to feel a change, a rearrangement in the heart's geography, when we find that our longings face not the mornings but the evenings, when our thirsting is for sleep, rest, peace, and not for the golden beginnings of the day. This at least is what I have now, and at this gathering together the bad times are over for me, and there is no more pain, and there are no more tears.

Judith was healed, though not cured.

Come to think of it, we can be healed at any time that we devote mind and heart to the task. Curing is a sometime thing. Healing is an everyday possibility—even an ordinary day can be a graceful event.

We waver between justice and mercy. Out of my memory comes a Biblical injunction: "to do justly (and) to love mercy. . . ." The drama of justice is played out every day in our courts. The need for a community, however large or small, to have some standards of behavior and some methods of dispensing justice to those who have violated those standards seems evident. Judging matters of right and wrong, handing out (or down) penalties for wrongdoing, and seeking to "make the punishment fit the crime" are essentials of justice. Needless to say, all dispensing of justice is approximate and errs regularly on both sides, severity and leniency. Gilbert and Sullivan commented penetratingly in words and music, "A policeman's lot is not a happy one!"

We also feel a need for mercy, for forgiveness, and for reconciliation. The recent South African effort has been bold in its conception and impressive in its actions. It incarnates a need beyond justice, the reknitting of the community's fabric to include those who have violated its standards and ruptured its vision of wholeness and inclusion. Mercy's aim lies beyond justice in redemption and the reconciliation of those who have become separated. It was this intuition that led Universalists of an earlier day to proclaim the nonexistence of Hell as the condition of absolute separation—beyond human and/or divine love and mercy.

A religion that claims for itself the mission of wholeness, of reconciliation, of universal redemption is challenged daily to move beyond justice toward mercy and the restoration of the human family to holiness and happiness. The partisans of justice are not wrong. The partisans of mercy seek to go a greater distance toward the wholeness our souls seek.

Every day we can see or read reports of justice, justice done, justice denied, justice ignored, justice exacted, and justice prostituted. And we hear demands for justice. We may even join in the chorus. It is a worthy endeavor. But it is not the last stop on the railroad, not the final goal. Even as we rejoice in justice achieved, we keep before us the goal beyond justice—the restoration of the whole fabric of community through mercy. The claim of mercy is a claim for all—for the judges as well as the judged, for victims as well as the victimizers.

I once saw an intriguing lecture topic: "Israel: Between Iraq and a Hard Place." It's a common problem. My name is Israel and I am everlastingly between Iraq and a hard place. It's ironic that our religion puts us in a hard place, where justice seems deserved and mercy undeserved, and that the way to wholeness beckons us toward the merciful way. Nobody said it would be easy.

My brother-in-law, in his retirement years, has become a clown. He joined a fraternal order's "clown group" and is learning the art of being a clown. The art seems to consist of exaggeration. Ordinary human traits are magnified or minimized to call attention to them. This allows us to laugh at ourselves in the guise of someone else. What a splendid contribution to human sanity: holding up the magnifying mirror to our humanness.

Most of us don't enjoy being laughed at. We take umbrage at it (even though umbrage upsets our stomachs). We take ourselves seriously, and we want others to take us (and themselves) seriously, too. It's hard, especially when grappling with a difficult problem or a crisis, to think of life as a joke. After a while we even begin to take seriously things that we believe. We are prepared to fight (even to the death, sometimes) to defend our notions. What a ministry it is, to magnify one's own notions to the point that their absurdity allows us the grace of saying, "It's possible I could be mistaken."

Our little planet orbits a rather small star, with (at last count) eight other planets, some even smaller, some much larger. Our modest solar system is one of thousands, perhaps millions, in our galaxy, the Milky Way galaxy. Our solar system is about 130,000 light years from the center of the galaxy. Light travels about 186,000 miles per second. A light year is the distance light travels in a year. Our galaxy, in turn, is one of a billion or two galaxies in the universe. These galaxies appear to be receding from one another at approximately the speed of light. This does throw a rather clownlike light on some of the claims made by religions for truth. We know very little, and we are not very certain of what we think we know for sure.

Yet in the face of the awesome dimensions of the universe, we keep trying to be kind to one another, modest about our attainments, and humble before life's magnificent intricacy, on which we are so completely dependent.

Maybe there is a little clown in each of us, helping us to remember how laughable some of our notions are, how small the island of knowledge, how long the shoreline of wonder, how brief our days, how vast our dwelling place. A chuckle now and then would probably not be amiss, especially when we see a clown, or a star.

I sometimes enjoy cooking. I've discovered that one of the greatest of culinary skills is making new creations out of leftovers. It takes imagination. It takes a little skill with spices, herbs, and sauces. The achievement of a satisfying and palatable meal from leftovers can be a model of how one might conduct one's own life in a creative way.

The first thing you need to do is to open the refrigerator door. You'll see an assortment of things: containers, jars, bags, boxes, and things wrapped in foil, waxed paper, or plastic.

Now I invite you to open a different door, the door of your past. What you find there will be leftovers, too. You will probably find your parents' voices, their admonitions, perhaps their praise, maybe their blame, their warnings, some expressions of their love, their anxiety. You may find traces of their uncertainties, problems, and hopes.

You will rediscover some decisions that you have made without thorough understanding of the consequences: about leaving home or not leaving; about when you decided to be married or not to be, or both, and to whom. You will probably remember some of the jobs you took, some of the jobs you wanted but didn't get, and some of the ones you thought about and turned down. You will also find some circumstances, accidents, diseases, and the times you were born into and lived through. You will find your family and some of its ways, its heritage, its customs, the habits that were funny or odd and are somehow deeply ingrained and make other ways seem even odder than your own. You will find people who touched your life in a thousand unaccounted and unexpected ways, who were there at special moments and changed you or made you a gift: the gift of a smooth stone, a happy day, or an unforgettable experience. And there will be all the ruins, sorrows, guilts, regrets, along with the fears and the hopes, dreams and doubts, forgivings and forbiddings. Don't we have crowded refrigerators! Everyone of us, such a collection of leftovers.

In making a life, we're all cooking with leftovers from childhood, even infancy. The longer we're at it, the more leftovers there are. Of course, people are always looking for the "big answer" and there is one big answer to cooking with leftovers. You open the door, and you are faced with the problem, What can I make of it? I take that to be the secret ingredient for dealing with leftovers. A scriptural version is "the substance of things hoped for, the evidence of things not seen." You might consider attaching it to the refrigerator door—either the internal one or the external one—since it's a description that fits both. What is that secret ingredient? It is, of course, faith. "Faith is the substance of things hoped for, the evidence of things not seen."

Welcome to the world where we all cook using leftovers—some of us with imagination, some with creativity, some merely resenting the task, some thinking there is no possibility in it. Add the secret ingredient. Something will come of it that will be at least edible, probably even palatable.

One of the common challenges of the ministry is to
be invited, usually without prior arrangement or even
notice, to grace a gathering with some religious
words, a prayer or some appropriate (and presumably
exalted) sentiment. When this happened to me again
recently (for the umpteenth time), I remembered
having written a prayer on the back of a calling card
one day when I got five minutes advance notice.
And, once I had used it and probably someone men-
tioned it afterwards, I put it in my wallet. So now it is
my wallet prayer, and if I have any suspicion or
inkling that one of those very-last-minute invitations
to pray out loud and in public and before who-knows-
what-faith varieties is imminent, I reach for my wallet and the little prayer. It's not exactly a prayer for all
occasions, but it does have a useful flexibility and
nonspecificity about it. The last time I used it was at
a meeting of ministers. A number of ministers, ever
alert for techniques, ploys, and other emergency
measures, asked about my wallet prayer, which surprised (as well as flattered) me. I suppose I thought
that all of us ministers had been the recipients of similar last-minute-please-help-me invitations and had,
therefore, devised similar defense strategies.

I do commend the strategy to any who (whether
clergy or laity) feel they may be invited to invoke the

Divine Presence or focus a moment's attention on life's larger dimensions. And, although it does not bear the Good Churchkeeping Seal of Approval, I've liked it well enough to keep it and to share it.

For simple things that are not simple at all
For miracles of the common way . . .
    Sunrise . . . Sunset
    Seedtime . . . Harvest
    Hope . . . Joy . . . Ecstasy
For Grace that turns
    our intentions into deeds
    our compassion into helpfulness
    our pain into mercy
For Providence that
    sustains and supports our needs
We lift our hearts in thankfulness
    and pray only to be more aware
    and thus more alive.

                            Amen

Sorry it's not wallet size.

It is no secret that winter is not my favorite season of the year. Oh, once upon a time I loved winter. I lived on a hill that was splendid for sledding. I had a very fast sled. There was opportunity for skiing and skating and making snow figures and snowballs. It was, as I look back upon it, quite pleasant; although I do remember some minor irritations such as long underwear and overshoes. But, taken together, the overall impression is a pleasant one.

As time passed, my impressions seem to have changed. Now I am anxious about such mundane matters as snow removal, the skyrocketing cost of heating, the perils of walking and driving on ice-covered streets, colds, flu, pneumonia, broken bones, sprains, strains, and bruises resulting from encounters with winter. I suppose these things happened to people during my childhood, too. I just didn't notice. It wasn't in my world then. Now winter is not my favorite. I like warm.

Last night I was nearly converted. It was snowing. I was driving to a meeting over streets paved, so it appeared, with diamonds. There was a brilliant sparkle to the snow as the headlights shone on it. As I looked more carefully, it seemed as though the reflections were of varied colors as well as that brilliant illumination for which *white* seems an inadequate word. A loveliness was showered on the landscape, roofs, trees, limbs, and asphalt, not to mention sundry uglinesses that had undergone a magical transformation into supernal beauty.

It wasn't less slippery for being supernal, and I imagine that some accidents resulted. It is hard to focus on the beauty when your car is sliding sideways or your body is deposited none too gently supine on the sidewalk.

But, for a while, I was almost converted by the beauty. In the world of hard and sometimes ugly reality, even half an hour on streets of diamonds is sustaining and beguiling.

O Thou Vast Life in which our little lives dwell
O Thou Spirit who art parent to our spirits
we rejoice in one great truth
    that our little lives can be partners in great
       enterprises
    that our little minds can contain great ideas
    that our little hearts can engender great hopes
    that our little spirits can conjure up great visions
    that our greatness is not of size, but of purpose
    that our strength is not of numbers, but of intent
    that our importance is not of duration, but of
       direction.

In the quiet and confidence of our own hearts
we have committed ourselves to holy orders
    to seek the holy in a world fragmented
    to seek peace in a world discontented
    to seek sanity in a world oft demented
    to seek health in a world oft tormented.
In our hearts we need great courage, lest it desert us
in peril.

In our minds are shining visions.
    Let them not be tarnished by the smothering fog
       of the traffic

and the obscuring mists of nay-sayings, doubts,
    and fears.

In our souls is the unquenchable impulse toward the
holy.
    Let it ever remind us that the ministry is
        about wholeness
        about healing
        about health.
Steel our wills to venture into dark, dismal, and
dreadful places.

May we hear the call to minister to the grieving
    the confused, the bewildered, the bruised
    the ecstatic and the gloomy
    the faithful and the faithless
    to the youngest, the oldest, and all the in-betweens
    to the noble, the ignoble
    and all the rest of us whose nobility is a sometime
        thing
    to the forbidding, the boring, and the forbearing
    to humans of every sort or condition.

We ministers (with or without portfolio or title) are
seekers
    after the holy wheresoever it is hidden
    to beckon it forth that it may shine
    with the ineffable splendor
    of human possibility and of human fulfillment.

Remind us, now and then, that such revelation is
    reward enough
    satisfaction enough
    paradise enough
    heaven enough.

And if, perchance, you are called "Reverend"
may you have the grace to smile, remembering that
you have been
    faithful to your calling
    persistent in your search for wholeness
    and committed to compassion for all.

Amen and amen

This list includes all meditation manuals published since the merger in 1961. For information about meditation manuals prior to 1961, contact Skinner House Books, 25 Beacon Street, Boston, MA 02108.

2000 *Glad to Be Human* Kaaren Anderson
      Out of the Ordinary Gordon B. McKeeman
1999 *The Rock of Ages at the Taj Mahal* Meg Barnhouse
      Morning Watch Barbara Pescan
1998 *Glory, Hallelujah! Now Please Pick Up Your Socks*
          Jane Ellen Mauldin
      Evening Tide Elizabeth Tarbox
1997 *A Temporary State of Grace* David S. Blanchard
      Green Mountain Spring and Other Leaps of Faith
          Gary A. Kowalski
1996 *Taking Pictures of God* Bruce T. Marshall
      Blessing the Bread Lynn Ungar
1995 *In the Holy Quiet of This Hour* Richard S. Gilbert
1994 *In the Simple Morning Light* Barbara Rohde
1993 *Life Tides* Elizabeth Tarbox
      The Gospel of Universalism Tom Owen-Towle
1992 *Noisy Stones* Robert R. Walsh
1991 *Been in the Storm So Long* Mark Morrison-Reed and
          Jacqui James, Editors
1990 *Into the Wilderness* Sara Moores Campbell
1989 *A Small Heaven* Jane Ranney Rzepka
1988 *The Numbering of Our Days* Anthony Friess Perrino

1987 *Exaltation* David B. Parke, Editor

1986 *Quest* Kathy Fuson Hurt

1985 *The Gift of the Ordinary* Charles S. Stephen, Jr., Editor

1984 *To Meet the Asking Years* Gordon B. McKeeman, Editor

1983 *Tree and Jubilee* Greta W. Crosby

1981 *Outstretched Wings of the Spirit* Donald S. Harrington

1980 *Longing of the Heart* Paul N. Carnes

1979 *Portraits from the Cross* David Rankin

1978 *Songs of Simple Thanksgiving* Kenneth L. Patton

1977 *The Promise of Spring* Clinton Lee Scott

1976 *The Strangeness of This Business* Clarke D. Wells

1975 *In Unbroken Line* Chris Raible, Editor

1974 *Stopping Places* Mary Lou Thompson

1973 *The Tides of Spring* Charles W. Grady

1972 *73 Voices* Chris Raible and Ed Darling, Editors

1971 *Bhakti, Santi, Love, Peace* Jacob Trapp

1970 *Beginning Now* J. Donald Johnston

1969 *Answers in the Wind* Charles W. McGehee

1968 *The Trying Out* Richard Kellaway

1967 *Moments of Springtime* Rudolf Nemser

1966 *Across the Abyss* Walter D. Kring

1965 *The Sound of Silence* Raymond Baughan

1964 *Impassioned Clay* Ralph Helverson

1963 *Seasons of the Soul* Robert T. Weston

1962 *The Uncarven Image* Phillip Hewett

1961 *Parts and Proportions* Arthur Graham